SCHIRMER'S LIBRARY
OF MUSICAL CLASSICS

Vol. 1170

Pasquale Bona

Professor in the Royal Conservatory of Milan

Rhythmical Articulation

A COMPLETE METHOD

Translated from the
Fourth Italian Edition, revised and
Augmented by the Author

By

DR. TH. BAKER

G. SCHIRMER, Inc.

DISTRIBUTED BY
HAL•LEONARD®
CORPORATION
7777 W. BLUEMOUND RD. P.O. BOX 13819 MILWAUKEE, WI 53213

PREFACE

The favorable reception and extraordinary success of my Method for Rhythmical Articulation (*Metodo per la Divisione*) have induced me to issue a Fourth Edition, which has been diligently revised, rearranged, and considerably augmented, and is now divided, for greater general convenience, into three parts, the first and second being for those who devote themselves to the study of singing, and all three for instrumentalists.

An incontestable proof of the utility of my work, aside from the favor and success which it has met with, is its adoption as a text-book by the best masters and by Schools of Music of the highest standing, such as the Conservatory at Milan.

The favor with which the former editions were received, appears to me no doubtful indication of the fortune that awaits this last one, which is certainly better than its predecessors.

P. BONA.

INTRODUCTION

If there is any one matter of special importance in musical education, it is doubtless to teach young pupils a practical method for the correct rhythmical proportionment of the single notes composing the beats of a musical theme, to recognize their respective time-values, and to give to each note, so to speak, a special significance and individuality, as considered in its interrelations with the rest.

Such teaching, known under the head of *Metodo per la Divisione* (Method for Rhythmical Articulation), has been decidedly neglected in former years in our Italian schools, being given only in large conservatories, in which, its great utility and importance being recognized, it has been adopted as an essential part of the instruction of young pupils, and is, therefore, regarded as one of the most important branches in the study of musical theory.*

It is unnecessary to dilate on the advantages flowing from a good method of rhythmical articulation, whether for recognizing the relations subsisting between the notes forming a musical beat, or for recognizing their individual character;—for enabling the executants to tell at a glance the time-values of the notes, which are sometimes grouped in such a manner as not to be readily distinguished by the eye, or for recognizing the different times (measures) in music, on the energy and precision of which depends the correct execution of the theme, which pupils find very difficult;—and, finally, for accustoming the pupil to effect with precision changes of time, a very hard thing to accomplish if he has not been thoroughiy drilled in the study of rhythmical articulation.

In consideration of all these advantages, I decided to publish the present Method, which, despite its modest appearance and proportions, contains every essential of a complete method of rhythmical articulation; and I venture to hope that my work will be favorably received, especially in view of the extremely flattering circumstance, that it has been adopted as a text-book in the Royal Conservatory at Milan.

* On the next page rhythmical articulation will be duly explained.

PRELIMINARY REMARKS

Before undertaking to read the First Part of this Method, it is necessary for the pupil to have learned the rudiments of musical theory; that he should know, above all, the time-values of the various notes and rests, common time, and the effect of the dot and the tie. For the Second Part he should be acquainted with all the different times, all the scales, and the irregular groups of notes (triplets, quintuplets, etc.; while he may defer to the Third Part a knowledge of everything which pertains to ligatures, embellishments, etc., etc.

Rhythmical articulation consists in pronouncing the name of each note *in the same manner as if one had to read the words,* but with the difference that the word must be sustained for the length of time indicated by the note named, and, in case the latter is longer than a quarter-note, the vowel must be repeated, keeping it connectedly sustained, as many times as there are quarter-notes contained in the note. To facilitate the movement of the tongue in groups of two, three, four or more notes, their several names should be pronounced flowingly and connectedly, as if reading a word composed of several syllables, taking care to emphasize the names of notes occupying strong beats.

With reference to all rests, a rest equal to a quarter-note is indicated by the word *uno* (one), one equal to two quarter-notes by *uno, due* (one, two), and so on, commencing with *uno* every time after the rest is interrupted by a note or falls on any other beat.* The word *uno* is likewise employed to distinguish the eighths among other notes. Time is beaten with the hand.

---

* All said above concerning the rests is not to be applied in practice until the pupil has learned the lesson, and, consequently, he will pause for the length of time indicated by the rests as they occur.

Illustrative Examples.

The figures 1, 2, 3, 4 indicate the quarters which constitute the beats, and the syllable Do‿o‿o‿o indicates the prolongation of the word pronounced, with a slight stress on each quarter. The words *uno, due, tre, quattro* (1, 2, 3, 4) serve to indicate the quarter-rests.

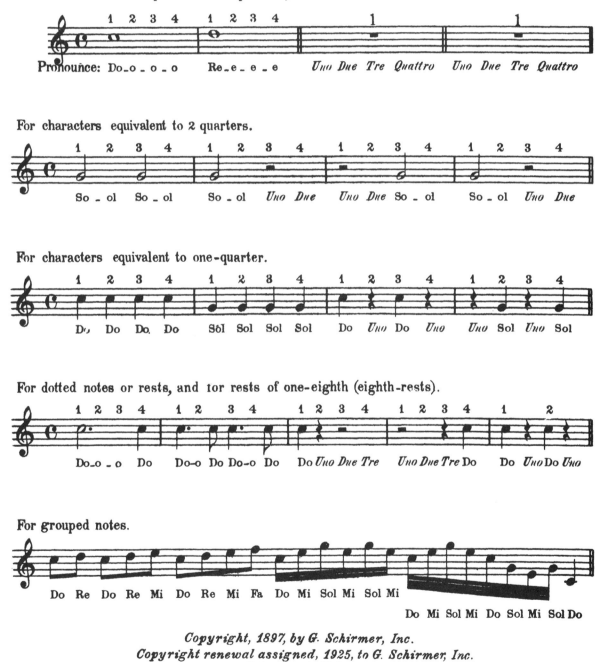

Scales exhibiting the names of the notes in all the clefs.

Violin-Clef.

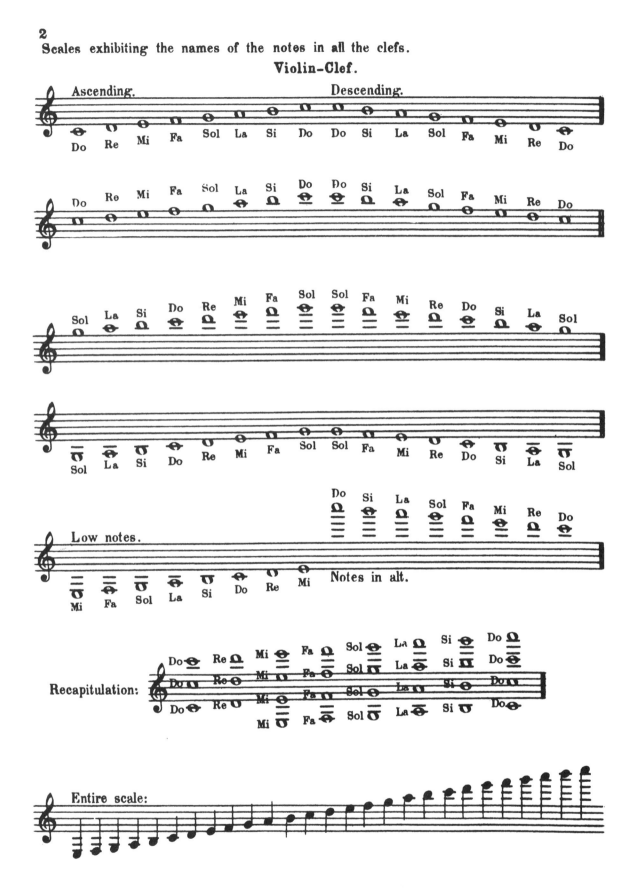

As soon as the pupil has become familiar with the names of the notes composing the first two scales, he may proceed to the reading of the First Part.

Bass–Clef.

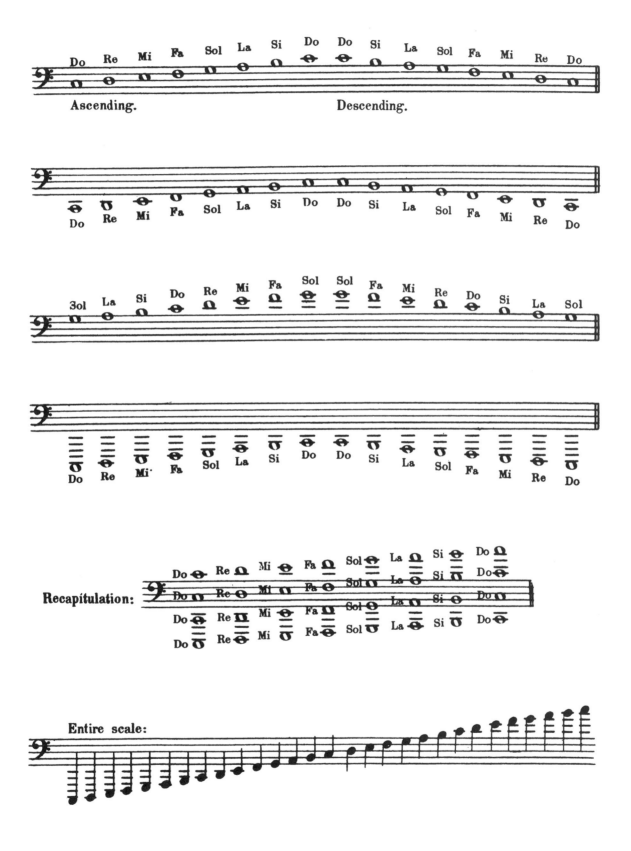

Ascending.   Descending.

Recapitulation:

Entire scale:

Tenor-Clef.

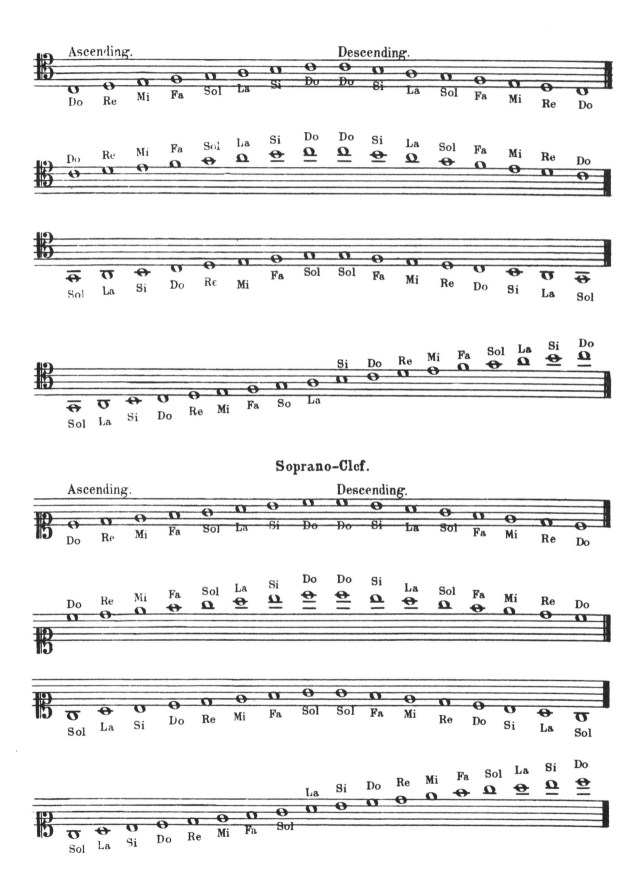

Soprano-Clef.

Mezzo-Soprano Clef.

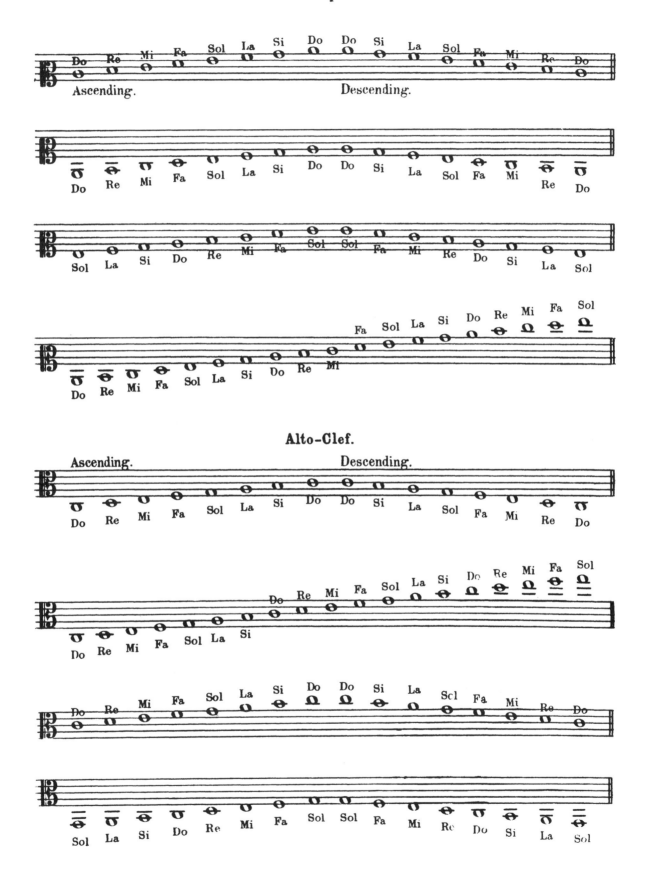

Baritone-Clef.

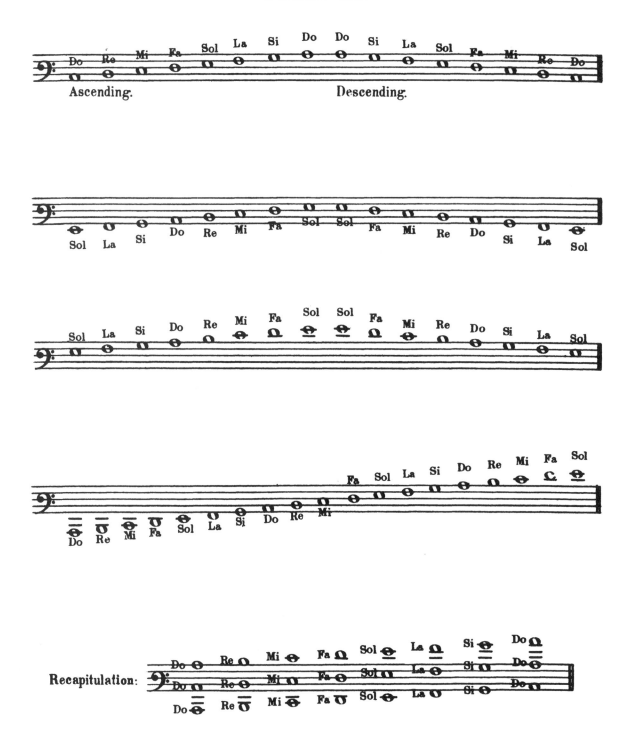

Ascending.   Descending.

Recapitulation:

This scale is added here in order that the pupil may learn the notes in this clef, of which he should make a reading-study; in which the present Method is written, although it is not proper to the same.

First Part.

8

Leaps of Thirds.

6.

The same.

7.

The same.

8.

Leaps of Fourths.

9.

The same.

10.

Little Solfeggi, or examples of notes interrupted by rests.

14

On the single dot.

The same.

54.

The same.

55.

The same.

56.

On the double dot.

57.

Mixed exercises.

58.

A tie connecting two notes of the same name or position shows that the second must not be repeated, but simply added to the first.

59.

Exercise on the single dot, **double dot, and tie**.

It is necessary that the teacher should make the pupil acquainted with the cases in which the dot, the tie, and the syncopation produce the same affect.

On Syncopation

Other examples according to the given rules.

18

Exercises on all the leaps, for the purpose of freeing the tongue before taking up the solfeggi of the Second Part.

69.

70.

71.

72.

Mixed leaps.

73.

Scales in 32nd notes.

74.

Second Part.

77. Andante.

28

Sostenuto.

89.

Moderato assai.

90.

Allegro.

91.

cresc.

Allegretto.

93.

a piacere   *dim.*

(a) Accent this well, and the cadence likewise.

Andante.

94.

Moderato assai.

95.

dim.   *a tempo*

Allegretto moderato assai.

96.

cresc.

Allegretto moderato.

98.

(a) Accent this well, and the cadence likewise.

Third Part.

This Part contains very nearly all combinations of rhythmical articulation, in the 8 ordinary times, with repeats and the abbreviations oftenest met with.

100. Allegretto.

Andante mosso.

101.

rall. *in tempo*

44

Allegro giusto.

104.

Allegro vivace.

107.

Adagio.

Andantino grazioso.

54

Moderato assai.

Moderato.

111.

Grave.

112. *con espressione*

58

cresc.

Allegretto.

113.

60

Allegro con brio.

115.

Sostenuto.

116.

64

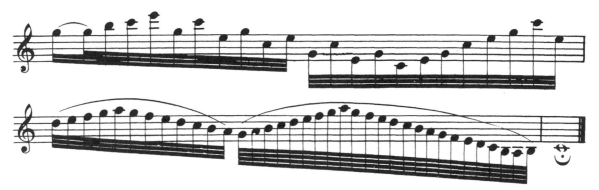

Exercises with signs of abbreviation and repeats.

Allegro mosso.

(a) In printed music, both these and the following abbreviations are seldom met with; this cannot be said of MS. music, hence, it is necessary to learn them.

Solfeggio for freeing the tongue.

Allegro spiritoso.

118.

Exercise on the other signs and abbreviations.

Allegro.

In this last solfeggio all the different times are represented, so as to accustom the pupil to change instantly.

Allegro moderato.